KID CHEFS

COOKING WITH GRAINS

Rose Miles

Enslow PUBLISHING

Please visit our website, www.enslow.com. For a free color catalog of all our high-quality books,
call toll free 1-800-398-2504 or fax 1-877-980-4454

Published in 2027 by
Enslow Publishing
2544 Clinton Street
Buffalo, NY 14224

Portions of this work were originally authored by Kristen Rajczak and published as Ingredients for a *Healthy Life: Fantastic Grain Recipes*. All new material in this edition is authored by Rose Miles.

Cataloging-in-Publication Data
Names: Miles, Rose.
Title: Cooking with grains / Rose Miles.
Description: Buffalo, NY : Enslow Publishing, 2027. | Series: Kid chefs | Includes glossary and index.
Identifiers: ISBN 9781978548572 (pbk.) | ISBN 9781978548589 (library bound) | ISBN 9781978548596 (ebook)
Subjects: LCSH: Cooking (Cereals)--Juvenile literature. | Grain--Juvenile literature.
Classification: LCC TX393.M674 2027 | DDC 641.331--dc23

Printed in China

Photos Credits: Cover, p. 1 itor/Shutterstock.com; cover, p. 1 Peter Hermes Furian/Shutterstock.com; cover, p. 1 ifiStudio/Shutterstock.com; cover, p. 1 baibaz/Shutterstock.com; cover, p. 1 Cook Shoots Food/Shutterstock.com; p. 4, 6, 8, 10, 12, 14, 16, 18, 20 ricorico/Shutterstock.com; p. 5 AYO Production/Shutterstock.com; p. 6 Public Domain/Public Domain; p. 7 New Africa/Shutterstock.com; p. 9 mujahid57/Shutterstock.com; p. 10 Peter Hermes Furian/Shutterstock.com; p. 11 AlexandrMusuc/Shutterstock.com; p. 12 Nataly Studio/Shutterstock.com; p. 13 grey_and/Shutterstock.com; p. 15 Aliking555/Shutterstock.com; p. 16 Deutschlandreform/Shutterstock.com; p. 17 uladzimir zgurski/Shutterstock.com; p. 18 Marcos Castillo/Shutterstock.com; p. 19 Prostock-studio/Shutterstock.com; p. 20 URem/Shutterstock.com; p. 21 TuktaBaby/Shutterstock.com

CPSIA compliance information: Batch #QSENS27: For further information, contact Enslow Publishing, New York, New York, at 1-800-398-2504.

Contents

Recipes in this book may use knives, mixers, and hot stove tops. Ask for an adult's help when using these tools.

Words in the glossary appear in **bold** type the first time they are used in the text.

A Healthy Breakfast

You probably know that breakfast is an important way to start the day. If you could eat anything you wanted for breakfast, what would you choose? Would you have a muffin, pancakes, or a big bowl of oatmeal? Or would you rather have your usual bowl of cornflakes? Whatever you'd pick, all these breakfast foods have something in common—they contain grains!

Grains are a big group of plants grown for food that are called cereal crops. Wheat, oats, and corn are just a few cereal crops. The grains people eat are the seeds of these crops. And they're quite tasty too!

Do You Have Allergies?

The **recipes** in this book may use **ingredients** that contain or have come into contact with nuts, gluten, dairy products, and other common causes of **allergies**. If you have any food allergies, please ask a parent or teacher for help when cooking and tasting!

Grains are a common part of a healthy, tasty ***diet****.*

Ancient Grains

People have been growing and eating grains for thousands of years. Barley may be the grain that's been grown the longest. It has a history of **cultivation** going back as many as 10,000 years! It's likely that both wheat and barley were first grown in an area in the Middle East, which includes parts of Egypt.

The ancient Egyptians grew wheat for dozens of different types of bread. Bread was an important part of their culture. It was very valuable and was even considered to have magical powers.

Tasty Tidbits

Wheat and loaves of bread are often seen in ancient Egyptian art and **hieroglyphs**.

Flour is one of the most common ways people eat grains. It can be used to make lots of different types of yummy breads.

Whole vs. Refined

Grain foods are usually placed in one of two categories: whole grains and refined grains.

Refined grains are when the grain seeds, or kernels, have been **processed**. The kernels may be cracked or broken into smaller pieces or pressed flat in giant rollers so they cook faster.

Whole grains are those that still contain the three main parts of the kernel: the bran, the germ, and the endosperm. Oats are a good example of a whole grain.

Tasty Tidbits

White flour, white bread, and most crackers are made with refined grains. That means the grain has been processed so much that it's lost many of its **nutrients**.

*Some breads use **yeast**, which can be time-consuming and hard to work with. This bread is a bit easier—that's why it's called a quick bread!*

Quick Bread with Oats

makes one loaf, about 10 servings

Ingredients:

1 cup old-fashioned rolled oats or quick-cooking oats, plus 2 tablespoons
1 ⅓ cups whole-wheat flour or white whole-wheat flour
1 cup all-purpose flour
2 ¼ teaspoons baking powder
¼ teaspoon baking soda
1 ¼ teaspoons salt
8 ounces low-fat plain yogurt
1 egg
¼ cup canola oil
¼ cup clover honey
¾ cup skim milk

Directions:

1. Preheat oven to 375 degrees.
2. Spray a bread loaf pan with cooking spray. Sprinkle 1 tablespoon of oats in the bottom of the pan. Shake the pan slowly from side to side to coat the sides and bottom of the pan with the oats.
3. Stir the whole-wheat and all-purpose flours together with the baking powder, baking soda, and salt.
4. In another bowl, use a fork to combine the remaining 1 cup of oats, yogurt, egg, oil, and honey. Blend in the milk.
5. Add the wet oat mixture to the flours until just mixed.
6. Pour the batter into the loaf pan. Sprinkle the last tablespoon of oats on the top.
7. Bake for about 40 to 50 minutes, or until a toothpick inserted into the middle comes out clean and the top is golden brown. Let it cool before eating.

Whole Grains are Best

The biggest part of the kernel is the endosperm. It's full of carbohydrates, **protein**, and some vitamins and minerals. The germ also contains protein, vitamins, and minerals, as well as healthy **fats**. Whole grains provide fiber, which is plant matter the body can't break down and uses to move food and waste through the body. Much of that is found in the bran.

When grains are refined, they commonly lose their bran and germ. So, about 25 percent of the kernel's protein is lost too. Eating whole grains whenever you can is the best choice for your diet.

Tasty Tidbits

Vitamins and minerals are nutrients the body needs to work well. While companies that make products with refined grains add some into their food, whole grains are a better source and have more protein and fiber.

All grains deliver carbohydrates, which the body uses for energy. But when eaten "whole," grains can give you so much more!

Check the Ingredients

If you're unsure about a grain product, check the ingredient list. The first ingredient should contain the word "whole." It could be whole-wheat or whole-grain flour. Some food products include a Whole Grain Stamp, which is an easy way to pick out these healthy foods.

Grain products, such as cereals, pastas, and breads, often have many ingredients. In addition to looking for those made with whole-wheat or whole-grain flour, choose grain products with a short ingredient list of things you recognize, like yeast, water, and milk.

Tasty Tidbits

It's easy to add whole grains to your diet. Eat a bran muffin instead of a pastry. Make whole-wheat toast instead of a plain bagel. Cook brown rice instead of white rice. Or choose whole-wheat pasta instead of regular.

Whole-Grain Party Mix

makes 8 cups

Ingredients:

4 cups whole-grain cereal (not flakes)
2 cups puffed brown rice cereal
1 cup sliced almonds
¼ cup raw sesame seeds
1 cup raw pumpkin seeds
1 tablespoon sesame oil
¼ cup soy sauce
1 tablespoon Worcestershire sauce
½ cup canola oil
½ teaspoon chili powder
¼ teaspoon salt

Serve this homemade whole-grain treat at your next party. Your friends will love trying something new and healthy!

Directions:

1. Preheat oven to 300 degrees.
2. Mix the whole-grain cereal, puffed rice cereal, almonds, sesame seeds, and pumpkin seeds together.
3. In a separate bowl, use a whisk or fork to blend the sesame oil, soy sauce, Worcestershire sauce, canola oil, chili powder, and salt.
4. Pour the liquid and spice mix over the cereal, almonds, and seeds. Toss to coat.
5. Spread the mixture onto a cookie sheet and bake for 30 minutes, stirring about every 10 minutes.
6. Remove from the oven and allow to cool and set before eating.

Bake It Up

Baking is one of the most fun ways to use grains! Whole-wheat flour instead of white flour is a great way to add some health benefits to your baked goods. It can give a yummy nutty flavor to pancakes, breads, and homemade crackers.

Sometimes whole-wheat flour can make baked goods too thick or heavy. One way to fix this is to use half whole-wheat and half white flour in a recipe. You're still getting the extra benefits of whole grain!

White whole-wheat flour is another great option for baked goods. It has the same nutritional benefits but gives baked goods a lighter flavor and **texture**.

Tasty Tidbits

Some recipes call for flour made from almonds, coconuts, or beans!

Sugar Cookies

makes about 2 dozen cookies, depending on size of cookie cutters

Ingredients:

1 cup white whole-wheat flour
½ cup all-purpose flour
1 teaspoon baking powder
¼ teaspoon salt

3 tablespoons butter
1 tablespoon canola oil
1 egg
½ cup light brown sugar
½ teaspoon vanilla extract

This recipe uses mostly whole-wheat flour, so you can have a treat that tastes good and is better for you too!

Directions:

1. Use a fork to mix together the flours, baking powder, and salt.
2. Melt the butter in a small pan on the stove. Heat until it's lightly browned, about 1 minute, stirring it a few times so that it doesn't burn. Remove from heat and let the butter cool slightly.
3. Mix together the browned butter, oil, egg, brown sugar, and vanilla.
4. Add the flour mixture to the wet ingredients a little at a time until well mixed.
5. Spread out a big sheet of plastic wrap. Make the dough into a ball and place it on the plastic wrap, and then wrap it up. Place the dough in the refrigerator for at least an hour.
6. Preheat oven to 350 degrees. Line two cookie sheets with parchment paper.
7. Sprinkle flour on the counter. Unwrap the dough and turn it out onto the flour.
8. Use a rolling pin to roll out the dough to about 1/8 inch thick. Cut out cookies with cookie cutters or an upside-down glass and place them on the cookie sheets.
9. Bake for 6 to 8 minutes, or until the edges look slightly brown.
10. Let the cookies cool for a few minutes before removing them from the sheets.

Better Barley

Depending on which grain you've chosen, whole grains can take 30 minutes to an hour to cook. Barley is a slow-cooking grain, but it's worth it! Alone, barley is chewy and nutty. You can eat it with vegetables or mix it with yogurt and fruit in place of oatmeal.

Barley is sold as flour, flakes, and, perhaps most commonly, in kernels. It's a good source of protein and fiber as well as two of the B vitamins.

Tasty Tidbits

Many whole grains can be eaten in ways similar to rice or pasta. But make sure you've got a quick-cooking kind or you have the time to prepare them!

Barley Salad

makes about 8 servings

The veggies in this recipe make it perfect for a dinner side dish or summer picnic salad.

Ingredients:

Salad:

3 cups vegetable stock
1 cup barley
½ cup onion, sliced thin
1 bunch radishes, sliced
1 cucumber, peeled, seeded, and diced
1 red bell pepper, seeded and sliced
1 large carrot, chopped small or grated
½ cup chopped fresh mint (or ¼ cup dried mint)
½ cup chopped fresh parsley

Dressing:

3 tablespoons extra-virgin olive oil
3 tablespoons fresh lemon juice
3–4 cloves garlic, mashed
pinch of salt

Directions:

1. Bring the vegetable stock to a boil in a pan on the stove. Add the barley and cover. Lower the heat and allow the barley to simmer for about 45 minutes, or until the stock has been mostly **absorbed**.
2. Drain the barley well. Place it in a bowl.
3. In another bowl, combine the extra-virgin olive oil, lemon juice, salt, and mashed garlic, and mix well.
4. Pour the dressing over the barley and stir to coat.
5. Allow the barley to cool. Then, add the onions, radishes, cucumber, red pepper, carrot, parsley, and mint. Stir together and chill in the refrigerator before serving.

Lots of Grains

There are so many kinds of grains out there to try! Spelt and farro are called "ancient grains" because they've been cultivated for so long.

Another group to try is known as "pseudograins." Amaranth is one popular pseudograin, as are quinoa (KEEN-wah) and buckwheat. These grains aren't in the same plant family as cereal grains, but are similar nutritionally and can be cooked in many of the same ways.

Tasty Tidbits

Corn is a grain too! And did you know that corn isn't just yellow? Throughout history, people have grown red, blue, pink, and even black corn!

A yummy bowl of popcorn while watching a movie means you're getting a serving of whole grains!

Gluten-Free

You've probably heard of foods being gluten-free. People with celiac disease can't eat wheat, barley, and rye products. Their body reacts badly to gluten, a protein found in these grains.

In a person with celiac disease, the small intestine is harmed by the body's reaction to gluten and can't properly absorb nutrients. While there's no cure for celiac disease, doctors have found that a gluten-free diet helps to manage the **digestive** problems the illness causes.

Tasty Tidbits

People with celiac disease can still chow down on grains like rice, corn, millet, and buckwheat.

Why Eat Grains?

Grains Make You Strong

- Whole grains are good sources of protein, which helps build muscle.

Grains Fill You Up

- Whole grains are full of fiber! That keeps your digestive system working well. And because fiber makes us feel full, eating grains can stop us from eating too much junk food.

Grains Boost Energy

- The carbohydrates in whole grains give the body energy, so you can get out there to run and play!

Grains Make You Feel Good

- Vitamins and minerals in whole grains provide the body with what it needs to grow and stay healthy.

Glossary

absorb: to take in

allergy: a body's sensitivity to usually harmless things in the surroundings, such as dust, pollen, or mold

cultivation: having to do with raising crops by caring for the land and plants as they grow

diet: the food one usually eats

digestive: having to do with the breaking down of food inside the body so it can be used

fat: one of the basic nutrients that supplies energy to the body

hieroglyphs: pictures and symbols that stand for words, used by ancient Egyptians as a system of writing

ingredient: a food that is mixed with other foods

nutrient: something a living thing needs to grow and stay alive

processed: changed from its original state

protein: a nutrient in many types of food that the body uses to grow, repair tissues, and stay healthy

recipe: an explanation of how to make food

texture: the structure, feel, and appearance of something

yeast: a product made of tiny fungi that help raise bread dough

Fact Check

1. Which is an example of a whole grain?
   a. oats
   b. white bread
   c. plain bagels

2. The biggest part of the kernel is the ____________.
   a. bran
   b. endosperm
   c. germ

3. Quinoa is a(n) ________.
   a. ancient grain
   b. pseudograin
   c. refined grain

Answers: 1. a, 2. b, 3. b

On the Internet

Kids Cooking for Life Recipes
www.kidscookingforlife.org/kcl-recipes/category/All+in+for+Whole+Grains
Check out lots more recipes to find new ways to get whole grains into your diet!

Making Bread Around the World
www.bbc.co.uk/bitesize/articles/zy78mbk#zc6s46f
Watch a video and learn about different types of bread eaten around the world. Then, test your knowledge with a short quiz.

Publisher's note to educators and parents: Our editors have carefully reviewed these websites to ensure that they are suitable for students. Many websites change frequently, however, and we cannot guarantee that a site's future contents will continue to meet our high standards of quality and educational value. Be advised that students should be closely supervised whenever they access the Internet.

Index